GENTLE HANDS

and Other Sing-Along Songs
for Social-Emotional Learning

Amadee Ricketts

Illustrated by Ashley Barron

free spirit
PUBLISHING®

Library of Congress Cataloging-in-Publication Data
Names: Ricketts, Amadee, 1973– author. | Barron, Ashley, illustrator.
Title: Gentle hands and other sing-along songs for social-emotional learning / Amadee Ricketts ; illustrated by Ashley Barron.
Description: Minneapolis, MN : Free Spirit Publishing, [2018] | Song lyrics with the tunes indicated.
Identifiers: LCCN 2017035995 (print) | LCCN 2017036988 (ebook) | ISBN 9781631982125 (ePub) | ISBN 9781631982118 (Web PDF) | ISBN 9781631982101 (hardcover) | ISBN 1631982109 (hardcover)
Subjects: LCSH: Children's songs—Texts.
Classification: LCC M1997 (ebook) | LCC M1997 .R5395 2018 (print) | DDC 782.42083—dc23
LC record available at https://lccn.loc.gov/2017035995

Edited by Brian Farrey-Latz
Cover and interior design by Shannon Pourciau

Printed in China

Free Spirit Publishing
An imprint of Teacher Created Materials
9850 51st Avenue North, Suite 100
Minneapolis, MN 55442
(612) 338-2068
help4kids@freespirit.com
freespirit.com

FSC
www.fsc.org
MIX
Paper | Supporting responsible forestry
FSC® C144853

CONTENTS

Songs

Gentle Hands

to the tune of "Frère Jacques"

Kind and gentle,
Kind and gentle,
Are my hands,
Are my hands.

Hands are made for holding,
Hands are made for clapping,
Gentle hands,
Gentle hands.

Kind and gentle,
Kind and gentle,
Are my feet,
Are my feet.

Feet are made for walking,
Feet are made for dancing,
Gentle feet,
Gentle feet.

Kind and gentle,
Kind and gentle,
Is my mouth,
Is my mouth.

Mouths are made for talking,
Mouths are made for singing,
Gentle mouth,
Gentle mouth.

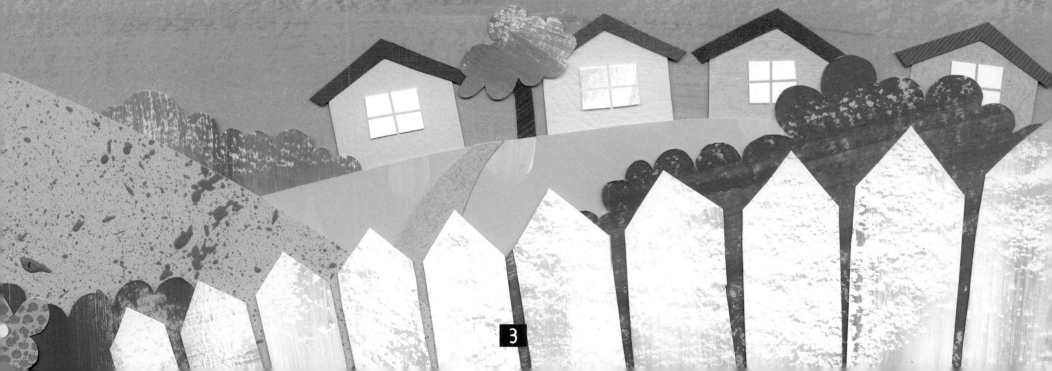

A-N-G-E-R

to the tune of "B-I-N-G-O"

When I feel mad, I take a break,
That's how I deal with anger.
A-N-G-E-R,
A-N-G-E-R,
Yes, I take a break,
That's how I deal with anger.

When I feel mad, I count to ten,
That's how I deal with anger.
A-N-G-E-R,
A-N-G-E-R,
Yes, I count to ten,
That's how I deal with anger.

When I feel mad, I take deep breaths,
That's how I deal with anger.
A-N-G-E-R,
A-N-G-E-R,
Yes, I take deep breaths,
That's how I deal with anger.

When I feel mad, I use my words,
That's how I deal with anger.
A-N-G-E-R,
A-N-G-E-R,
Yes, I use my words,
That's how I deal with anger.

My Body Belongs to Me

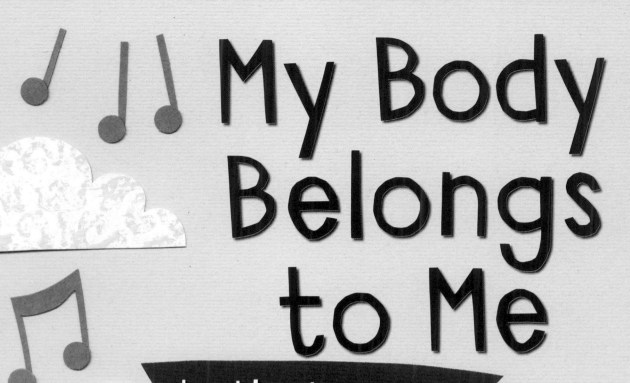

to the tune of

"99 Bottles of Pop on the Wall"

I am in charge of my body,
My body belongs to me.
My eyes, my nose, my fingers and toes,
My body belongs to me.

I take good care of my body,
My body belongs to me.
I eat good food and get lots of rest,
My body belongs to me.

I take good care of my body,
My body belongs to me.
I run and play, and exercise,
My body belongs to me.

I am in charge of my body,
My body belongs to me.
My eyes, my nose, my fingers and toes,
My body belongs to me.

It's OKAY to Ask for HELP

to the tune of "I'm a Little Teapot"

8

I can do a lot of things myself,
But sometimes I must ask for help.
Whether you're a grown-up,
Or just turned three,
It's okay to say, "Please help me."

9

HAPPY

ANGRY

I Have Feelings

to the tune of

"Twinkle, Twinkle, Little Star"

SAD

CONFUSED

SURPRISED

SCARED

I have feelings,
So do you.
Everyone
Has feelings, too.

When I'm kind,
And help, and share,
All my friends
Will know I care.

I have feelings,
So do you.
Everyone
Has feelings, too.

DISGUSTED

EMBARRASSED

Everybody Makes MISTAKES

to the tune of "London Bridge Is Falling Down"

Sometimes I'm Scared

to the tune of "Miss Mary Mack"

14

Sometimes I'm scared, scared, scared.
I feel afraid, 'fraid, 'fraid.
But I know, know, know,
I'll be okay, 'kay, 'kay.

When I feel scared, scared, scared,
I like a light, light, light,
And then I know, know, know,
I'll be all right, right, right.

When I feel scared, scared, scared,
I hug my bear, bear, bear,
And then I know, know, know,
Somebody cares, cares, cares.
When I feel scared, scared, scared,

I'll ask for help, help, help.
Then I won't be, be, be,
All by myself, self, self.

Sometimes I'm scared, scared, scared.
I feel afraid, 'fraid, 'fraid.
But I know, know, know,
I'll be okay, 'kay, 'kay.

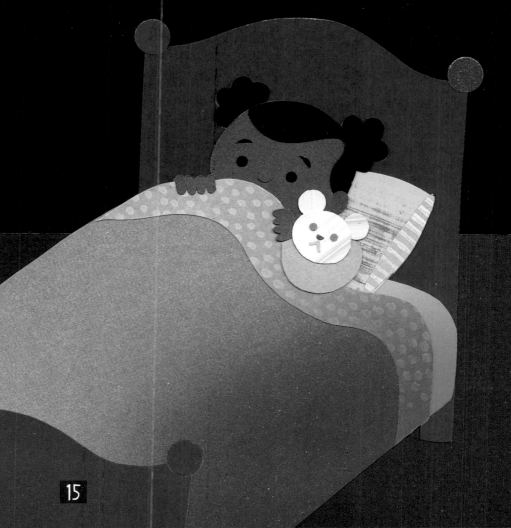

15

Should We Be Quiet or Loud Now?

to the tune of "The Bear Went Over the Mountain"

Should we be quiet or loud now?
Should we be quiet or loud now?
Should we be quiet or loud now?
Let's look around and see.

I use a quiet voice inside,
I use a quiet voice inside,
I use a quiet voice inside,
So everyone can hear.

(Softer and softer)

So everyone can hear,
So everyone can hear.

I use a quiet voice inside,
So everyone can hear.

Shhhhh.

I use a louder voice outside,
I use a louder voice outside,
I use a louder voice outside,
And everyone has fun!

(Louder and louder)

And everyone has fun,
And everyone has fun.

I use a louder voice outside,
And everyone has fun!

Hooray!

Should we be quiet or loud now?
Should we be quiet or loud now?
Should we be quiet or loud now?
Let's look around and see.

Listening Ears

to the tune of "Happy Birthday"

Time for listening ears,
Time for listening ears.
Put your ears on, everybody,
Time for listening ears.

Put your hands in your lap,
Put your hands in your lap.
Time for calm, quiet hands now,
Put your hands in your lap.

Time for listening ears,
Time for listening ears.
Put your ears on, everybody,
Time for listening ears.

Playing Is More Fun with EVERYONE

to the tune of "She'll Be Coming 'Round the Mountain"

We know playing is more fun with everyone,
Yes, playing is more fun with everyone.
Our playtime is much better when we all join in together,
Because playing is more fun with everyone.

We know playing is more fun with everyone,
Yes, playing is more fun with everyone.
When everyone's invited, then we all can get excited,
Because playing is more fun with everyone.

We know playing is more fun with everyone,
Yes, playing is more fun with everyone.
It's more fun without a doubt when nobody feels left out,
Because playing is more fun with everyone.

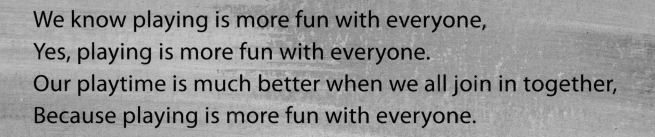

If You're a GOOD FRIEND and YOU KNOW IT

to the tune of
"If You're Happy and You Know It"

If you're a good friend and you know it, wave hello.
If you're a good friend and you know it, wave hello.
If you're a good friend and you know it,
Then your friendly wave will show it.
If you're a good friend and you know it, wave hello!

If you're kind and you know it, give a hug.
If you're kind and you know it, give a hug.
If you're kind and you know it,
Then a great big hug will show it.
If you're kind and you know it, give a hug.

If you're a helper and you know it, lend a hand.
If you're a helper and you know it, lend a hand.
If you're a helper and you know it,
Then your helping hands will show it.
If you're a helper and you know it, lend a hand.

If you're caring and you know it, share your toys.
If you're caring and you know it, share your toys.
If you're caring and you know it,
Sharing toys will always show it.
If you're caring and you know it, share your toys.

If you're a good friend and you know it, wave goodbye.
If you're a good friend and you know it, wave goodbye.
If you're a good friend and you know it,
Then your friendly wave will show it.
If you're a good friend and you know it, wave goodbye!

I Am THANKFUL

to the tune of "Oh My Darling, Clementine"

I am thankful, I am thankful,
I am thankful, right now.
I am feeling very thankful,
I am thankful right now.

For my home and for my family,
And for being safe and warm.
Right now I am feeling thankful,
I am thankful right now.

Are you thankful, are you thankful,
Are you thankful, right now?
Tell me why you're feeling thankful,
Why you're thankful right now.

TIPS FOR PARENTS AND CAREGIVERS

Gentle Hands is meant to be shared anywhere, any time, one on one, or with a group. The individual songs are short and simple enough to fit right into your routine. Whether it is bedtime, storytime, classroom time, circle time, or stuck-in-traffic time, these songs are a fun way to share social-emotional skills with young children.

Talk About It

The social-emotional concepts in this book come up throughout the day at home and at school. Each of these moments is a chance to talk about feelings, kindness, inclusion, or being a good friend. Seeing the way these general ideas fit in to their own experiences helps young children make connections between ideas and actions.

Just as specific praise ("It was really kind when Marcus offered Serena a turn playing with the train") is more meaningful than general praise ("Marcus is kind"), specific moments provide an opportunity for meaningful discussion ("Thank you for telling me that you are feeling afraid. Talking about it can help! Can you think of any other things that might help when you are feeling scared?").

Singing and Learning

Songs are a great way to teach new words and concepts, in part because they are so easy to remember. One great example is the alphabet song. (Because I mentioned it, you are probably thinking of the tune right now!) Advertising jingles are less educational, but a good jingle "sticks" in your head. This demonstrates the powerful connection between music and memory.

Familiar tunes like the ones in this book, which come from nursery rhymes and folk songs, are easy for anyone to sing and remember. Whether you think of yourself as a singer or not, the children you care for love to hear your voice simply because it is yours. Singing together is a wonderful way to bond.

Along with teaching new concepts and providing special time together, singing is valuable for young children because it helps them hear and differentiate between the smaller sounds that make up words. This skill is an important building block when children begin learning to read.

One of the most effective ways to share the early learning benefits of singing is also the simplest: sing the same songs again and again. Just as small children enjoy revisiting a familiar story or a favorite toy, the confidence that comes with repetition is clear when singing a special song together with a child who knows the words and the tune. Once your child or group really knows a song, you can add interest by changing it up a little. Try varying the pace ("Can we sing it slowly? How about reeeeeeally slooowly?"), or the volume, as in "Should We Be Quiet or Loud Now?" Hearing a song in a different way can help kids focus on the words and the way the words and the tune work together.

Another way to get the most out of singing together is to play with rhyming lyrics. Rhymes help children hear the smaller sounds in words, just as songs do. So, songs that rhyme are especially effective early learning tools. With older children (four and five years old), it is fun to talk about rhymes and work together to find rhyming words. For instance, in "I Have Feelings," there are two pairs of rhyming words: you and too, and care and share. You may be surprised at how many more "oo" words and "air" words children can identify when they start thinking about it.

Once you have some additional rhyming words, try them out in the song:

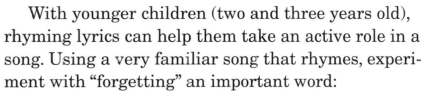

> When I'm kind,
> And help, and share,
> All my friends
> Will know *I'm a chair.*
> ... *I'm hair.*
> ... *I'm a bear.*
> ... *I'm fair.*

Do the new words make sense? Are they silly? This game works best if there are no "wrong" answers, just funny ones.

With younger children (two and three years old), rhyming lyrics can help them take an active role in a song. Using a very familiar song that rhymes, experiment with "forgetting" an important word:

> When I'm kind,
> And help, and share,
> All my friends
> Will know I _____

(Make a puzzled face, giving kids a chance to fill in the missing word.)

Interactive Storytime Fun

Although they have a wide application in several different settings, the songs in this book were written with storytime in mind. A successful storytime is interactive, inclusive, and fun. The way that looks varies from group to group and day to day, but it rarely features young children sitting still and being passive listeners for more than a minute or two at a time. And it shouldn't! Small children have lots of energy and short attention spans. It's best to plan activities to work with those characteristics, not in spite of them.

Learning to pay attention and be part of a group are important. But flexibility and an awareness of each child's unique developmental needs are just as important. If a behavior does not harm anyone or actively interfere with other children's learning, err on the side of being adaptable. Some children learn best while sitting still and listening. Others may need to keep moving, whether that means holding a fidget, standing up, or even dancing around.

One way to help children calm down and focus on storytime is to start with a welcome song, like "Listening Ears," or another familiar tune. Using the same opening song each time creates a special routine and a sense of anticipation. Knowing what to expect helps kids get ready to listen. Of course, different children listen differently, and not every child will follow the directions in the song. That's okay! The goal is to create a calm, welcoming environment that gives each child a chance to engage in his or her own way.

Adding interactive elements to storytime is a great way to keep kids engaged. Some simple ways to make storytime interactive are:

Add songs, rhymes, and transition activities between books. For instance, after reading a story you might lead the group in a song like "Gentle Hands," or another song that relates to the themes in the story you just read. After the next story, try a familiar rhyme or song that offers a chance to move around, like "If You're Happy and You Know It." For groups that are especially young or wiggly, it sometimes works best to spend as much time on transitions as you do on stories.

Encourage active participation. Many picture books and children's songs have participatory elements built in, like "The Itsy-Bitsy Spider." Many others lend themselves to participatory reading. Emphasize repeated words or phrases the children can say with you. Create motions or gestures that go with the text. If the text has a rhythm to it, tap it out so children can tap along. For example, in the song "Head, Shoulders, Knees, and Toes," children are encouraged to tap the part of the body in time with the song. In this book, you might add gestures

to a song like "Gentle Hands." Children can wiggle their hands when hands are mentioned, tap their feet at the mention of feet, and point to their mouths during the verse about mouths.

Embrace repetition. Young children love knowing what to expect and having a chance to show what they know. Let the interests of the group be your guide, revisiting songs and stories that spark their interest and moving on from those that do not. For instance, if your child enjoys singing, "If You're a Good Friend and You Know It" more than another song, go ahead and sing it again!

Practice dialogic reading. This means asking open-ended questions about the text, pictures, or themes in a book, and giving children a chance to answer. For example, after reading a book about a character who feels angry or after singing "A-N-G-E-R," you might ask, "Can you tell me about a time you were angry? What did you do?" Dialogic reading is fairly straightforward when reading with one or two children but tougher when reading with a group. Try starting off with questions that are not open-ended. Asking for yes, no, or single-word answers gives children a chance to take turns speaking and listening. Then you can continue with the story. As children get comfortable with this pattern, experiment with asking more open-ended questions. For example, you might graduate from, "Does the little girl in the story look angry?" to "How do you think she is feeling?" With practice, this technique can make storytime more fun and inclusive.

About the Author

Amadee Ricketts received her MLS degree from the College of St. Catherine and has been a librarian since 2002. She is currently the library director at the Cochise County Library District in Arizona. When not working or writing, she enjoys taking photos of insects and other tiny things. She lives with her husband, who is a photographer, and their cat.

About the Illustrator

Ashley Barron is an illustrator who specializes in paper collage. A graduate of the Ontario College of Art & Design's illustration program, her work has appeared in magazines, books, apparel, ad campaigns, animations, set designs, and window displays. Her illustrated books include the Math in Nature series, *Kyle Goes Alone* and *Up!* (Owlkids), and *Birthdays Around the World* (Kids Can Press). Originally from Whitby, Ashley now lives in Toronto with her partner Kevin, their three cats, and a parrot.

For free downloads—including simple sheet music and sound files—visit freespirit.com/gentlesongs.